She Holds a Cosmos

She Holds a Cosmos

Poems on Motherhood

Edited by Mallory Farrugia

Foreword by Kimiko Hahn

Illustrations by Karolin Schnoor

CHRONICLE BOOKS
SAN FRANCISCO

Library of Congress Cataloging-in-Publication Data

Names: Farrugia, Mallory, editor. | Hahn, Kimiko, 1955- author of
foreword. | Schnoor, Karolin, illustrator.
Title: She holds a cosmos : poems on motherhood / edited by Mallory
Farrugia ; foreword by Kimiko Hahn ; illustrations by Karolin Schnoor.
Description: San Francisco : Chronicle Books, [2021] |
 Includes bibliographical references. | Summary: "A collection of po-
ems about the experience of being a mother"—Provided by publisher.
Identifiers: LCCN 2020040812 | ISBN 9781797209890 (hardcover) |
ISBN 9781797211497 (ebook)
Subjects: LCSH: American poetry. | Motherhood—Poetry. |
Mother and child—Poetry. | LCGFT: Poetry.
Classification: LCC PS595.M64 S54 2021 |
DDC 808.81/93525—dc23
LC record available at https://lccn.loc.gov/2020040812

Manufactured in China.

Design by Vanessa Dina.
Typeset in Albra and BR Hendrix.

10 9 8 7 6 5 4 3 2 1

Chronicle books and gifts are available at special quantity discounts
to corporations, professional associations, literacy programs, and
other organizations. For details and discount
information, please contact our premiums department at
corporatesales@chroniclebooks.com or at 1-800-759-0190.

Chronicle Books LLC
680 Second Street
San Francisco, California 94107
www.chroniclebooks.com

CONTENTS

Mothering

by Kimiko Hahn

My granddaughter, just two, sits at the counter and demands paper and pencil. She sees my daughter—her mother—writing up a grocery list and wants to do the same. She scribble-scrabbles and says, "Fish, bubbles, train." I finish clearing lunch plates.

We are sequestered and running out of paper napkins. I cut three dish cloths in half and hem them on my mother's 1950 sewing machine. Just recalling how to thread the bobbin is a tiny domestic triumph. The project takes care of a rumble, a disquiet larger than the modest task.

On a bus, I bump into a former student. She tells me that she's distraught, not sure how to move forward. She is not sure she wants to be an elementary school teacher, but equally unsure what else to do. I ask her, "What are your options?" I listen. She admits that she's never said all this aloud before. I recall a teacher I had who just listened to me, and how that moment became a way of listening to myself. How *like a mother*, that teacher of mine was. All the different feelings about the word *mother* beg the exploration: *What is mother and what is mothering?*

At an earlier time in my life, I thought I knew very well what *mother* meant. And, young and fixed as I was in my view, the definition would surely have been limited. I'd have started with the biological definition: *a woman who has given birth*. Then I'd have included: *raising offspring*. It was simple. The suburbs in the 1960s would stay simple a little longer; around me the sitcoms broadcast on TV would set the paradigm. The images would also prompt my abiding disquiet. Looking back, change was the air we breathed, and the perceived limits of mother-hood would soon be broken through.

What else is *mother*? Of course, even then, a definition would extend to adoption. There were women who'd raise children to whom they hadn't given birth—but, in a splendidly alternate sense, had given life. Yes, there were couples in our neighbor-hood who "couldn't have children," so they adopted babies; others who welcomed orphans into their already large brood. In that bygone era, there was a sense of adding a necessary puzzle piece in order to make a complete family.

My own situation reflects what would have been considered the norm: I am a mother of two daughters and the grandmother of a girl and a boy—and of course I had a mother, long since wrested away from me, figuratively and literally. Perhaps in spite of that paradigm, my views have evolved and keep evolving. Against conventional views, I've come to see how *mothering* takes fur-ther forms. Some women give birth but do not mother. Some donate eggs—the biological component of motherhood—and may never see the offspring. Others have children with whom they are biologically connected, although a surrogate carried and delivered the baby. There are people who identify as male, give birth, and parent (or not). There are families with two mothers. There are "blended families."

There are moments (like this morning, chatting on the phone with a daughter one hundred miles away), when I pause and feel surprised that *I am a mother*. I wonder to myself, *Who are you?* Then, *Was I good enough?* I admit that I am not completely certain what a *mother* is in this still-new millennium, let alone what it means to *mother*.

Yes, apart from *mother*, there is *motherhood*, a circumstance that is more complicated than definition or belief or updates. The state of being is, literally and symbolically, a matrix.

> *Matrix*—late Middle English (in the sense of "womb"): from Latin, "breeding female," later "womb," from *mater, matr-*; "mother"—is an environment or material in which something develops.

I like that the etymology suggests a condition that, in my mind, can be as fraught as it can be jubilant. I recall during the heavy final months of pregnancy the increasingly panicky realization that the cervix (if all went as the midwife said) would dilate from pencil-point to centimeters wide for the crowning. With the arrival of the little interloper, a new panic would take up permanent residence and alter my being.

Ancillary to the question *What is* mother? is *Who gets to define the position?* Or, for our purposes, *Who gets to write the poem?*

I revel in the range of voices in this anthology. I personally believe that the mothers' points of view are foremost. I know that writing poetry about motherhood is not new (Sappho was a mother!). But the availability, the interest, and the numerous expressions are, dare I say, revolutionary. Why? When one is not permitted creativity, just expressing oneself is radical. That women's points of view are paramount comes from hard experience: I recall a male writer reviewing my early poems on the birth of my children. He criticized my poems by remarking that they were not joyous like other women's; my poems were like "crumbs under a rug." Really? Who is he to dictate how a woman should write about her experiences? Birth is messy and painful. Am I not *allowed* to express that primal experience? The male critic attempted censorship.

Who are you? . . . Was I a good enough mother? This anthology feels like a wonderful means to explore matrixes. There are poems from soon-to-be mothers. In Toi Derricotte's "In Knowledge of Young Boys," the woman imagines the baby as "newt-like"; in Elizabeth Spires's "Letter in July," a tiny being prepares to exit carrying a lantern; Mina Loy in "Parturition" writes of pain that is so intensely different from all other experiences that it becomes "exotic" and a "Negation of myself" (so true!). Above all, there is a realization of survival and the opening of a new chapter.

After "arrival," however the baby has entered into the home, what next? One thing I have known since I babysat in high school: Babies do not arrive with instructions. So, where does one, the birth or adoptive or surrogate mother, find instruction for the act of mothering? Most pieces of advice are handed down, by gesture and example. There are any number of books and blogs; for me, one of the most enduring words of wisdom (a manifesto, so to speak) came from Dr. T. Berry Brazelton: "The goal of attachment is detachment." Then again, much guidance arrives from word of mouth. The best advice I ever heard was from a single mother: "Surround your child with people you love and who love you too." Yes, it is possible for the child to feel loved and become empathetic in turn. On the other hand, there is also observing what one might call negative examples—vowing never to be like the mother who, say, leashes her toddler for a stroll on a busy street.

Poems offer plenty of room for exploring emotional complexities. Emily Pérez in "We Cannot Sleep Alone" admits to calling the son "my love, my tiny enemy." Kate Baer in "Motherload" remarks that the mother holds the child's ego. In Jennifer Givhan's "Prayer," the mother will make no bargain with God to let the son be taken. Louise Glück's "A Fable" is not surprisingly colored with potential violence and claim. And, after all is given over, what more can one give, or, really: *Do I never give enough? Why does love arrive with such exacting doubt?* In all this, there are more questions even for the responsible adult: *What has happened to me? To my body? Where has my body gone to and will I ever retrieve or recognize it?* Yes and no.

Then there is the child's point of view, where *mother* runs the gamut from Absolute Love Object to Absolute Restraint. She is the quintessential Other, the one from whom we first part bodily, then, with increasing frequency and distance, separate symbolically. In her poem, Lucille Clifton's mama "moved among the days." In "Nature, the gentlest mother," Emily Dickinson views the figure as the grand allegory of Mother Nature. But at the end of the day, as David Young recalls for us in "Mother's Day," mother is working. Yes, she is cooking stew, kissing hurts, attaching water-wings to little limbs, leaving home to work. And she is returning for the second shift, making sense of tumult and play.

Over the decades my image of *mothering* has changed as my sense of what being a mother means has changed and as I realize new aspects. I am pleased to go beyond the convention that limits mothering to the birth mother or primary caregiver. And, really, the definition of *motherhood* describes it as a state of being, not a gender or an office. Indeed, anyone can possess a maternal impulse.

If we can see *mothering* as a potential in us all, then these poems will be experienced in a prismatic way. If we can use *mother* as verb, everyone is enjoined to identify with raising a child. Everyone is welcome to claim the happiness and admit the difficult times. Poems are, after all, not merely for the head; nor are they just for the heart. Poems, especially these poems, offer beautiful risk-taking, a means to explore matrixes.

Letter in July

Elizabeth Spires

My life slows and deepens.

I am thirty-eight, neither here nor there.

It is a morning in July, hot and clear.

Out in the field, a bird repeats its quaternary call,

four notes insisting, *I'm here, I'm here.*

The field is unmowed, summer's wreckage

   everywhere.

Even this early, all is expectancy.

It is as if I float on a still pond,

drowsing in the bottom of a rowboat,

curled like a leaf into myself.

The water laps at its old wooden sides

as the sun beats down on my body,

a wand, an enchantment, shaping it

into something languid and new.

A year ago, two, I dreamed I held

a mirror to your unborn face and saw you,

in the warped watery glass, not as a child

but as you will be twenty years from now.

I woke, a light breeze lifting the curtain,

as if touched by a ghost's thin hand,

light filling the room, coming from nowhere.

I know the time, the place of our meeting.

It will be January, the coldest night

of the year. You will be carrying a lantern

as you enter the world crying,

and I cry to hear you cry.

A moment that, even now,

I carry in my body.

In Knowledge of Young Boys

Toi Derricotte

i knew you before you had a mother,

when you were newtlike, swimming,

a horrible brain in water.

i knew you when your connections

belonged only to yourself,

when you had no history

to hook on to,

barnacle,

when you had no sustenance of metal

when you had no boat to travel

when you stayed in the same

place, treading the question;

i knew you when you were all

eyes and a cocktail,

blank as the sky of a mind,

a root, neither ground nor placental;

not yet

red with the cut nor astonished

by pain, one terrible eye

open in the center of your head

to night, turning, and the stars

blinked like a cat.   we swam

in the last trickle of champagne

before we knew breastmilk—we

shared the night of the closet,

the parasitic

closing on our thumbprint,

we were smudged in a yellow book.

son, we were oak without

mouth, uncut, we were

brave before memory.

The Art of Creation

Patience Agbabi

I

Teardrop in a teat pipette,

my fate lies in the litmus:

pink or blue.

II

My secret garden's in bud but

I can't stand the smell of red roses.

III

All night

I dream of morning sickness.

All day I crave nutritious sleep.

IV

I'm eating crab apples

as if an anaconda

sold them to me.

V

My child shall inherit the earth.

I swallow grains at dusk

sweet with dew.

VI

Baby's treadmilling my belly.

They learn to run before they can walk.

VII

I shall breastfeed.

I shall front crawl myself fit.

I long to see my feet.

VIII

Our first, real conflict.

One of us wants to go out,

the other, to sleep.

IX

My mind, my body

open, a fist unclenching.

Then I hear her cry.

Parturition

Mina Loy

I am the centre

Of a circle of pain

Exceeding its boundaries in every direction

The business of the bland sun

Has no affair with me

In my congested cosmos of agony

From which there is no escape

On infinitely prolonged nerve-vibrations

Or in contraction

To the pin-point nucleus of being

Locate an irritation   without

It is   within

                       Within

It is without

The sensitized area

Is identical   with the extensity

Of intension

I am the false quantity

In the harmony of physiological potentiality

To which

Gaining self-control

I should be consonant

In time

Pain is no stronger than the resisting force

Pain calls up in me

The struggle is equal

The open window is full of a voice

A fashionable portrait-painter

Running up-stairs to a woman's apartment

Sings

    "All the girls are tid'ly did'ly

    All the girls are nice

    Whether they wear their hair in curls

    Or—"

At the back of the thoughts to which I permit crystallization

The conception   Brute

Why?

    The irresponsibility of the male

Leaves woman her superior Inferiority.

He is running up-stairs

I am climbing a distorted mountain of agony

Incidentally with the exhaustion of control

I reach the summit

And gradually subside into anticipation of

Repose

Which never comes

For another mountain is growing up

Which   goaded by the unavoidable

I must traverse

Traversing myself

Something in the delirium of night-hours

Confuses while intensifying sensibility

Blurring spatial contours

So aiding elusion of the circumscribed

That the gurgling of a crucified wild beast

Comes from so far away

And the foam on the stretched muscles of a mouth

Is no part of myself

There is a climax in sensibility

When pain surpassing itself

Becomes Exotic

And the ego succeeds in unifying the positive and negative poles
of sensation

Uniting the opposing and resisting forces

In lascivious revelation

Relaxation

Negation of myself as a unit

    Vacuum interlude

I should have been emptied of life

Giving life

For consciousness in crises   races

Through the subliminal deposits of evolutionary processes

Have I not

Somewhere

Scrutinized

A dead white feathered moth

Laying eggs?

A moment

Being realization

Can

Vitalized by cosmic initiation

Furnish an adequate apology

For the objective

Agglomeration of activities

Of a life.

LIFE

A leap with nature

Into the essence

Of unpredicted Maternity

Against my thigh

Tough of infinitesimal motion

Scarcely perceptible

Undulation

Warmth   moisture

Stir of incipient life

Precipitating into me

The contents of the universe

Mother I am

Identical

With infinite Maternity

    Indivisible

    Acutely

    I am absorbed

    Into

The was—is—ever—shall—be

Of cosmic reproductivity

Rises from the subconscious

Impression of a cat

With blind kittens

Among her legs

Same undulating life-stir

I am that cat

Rises from the sub-conscious

Impression of small animal carcass

Covered with blue-bottles

—Epicurean—

And through the insects

Waves that same undulation of living

Death

Life

I am knowing

All about

    Unfolding

The next morning

Each woman-of-the-people

Tip-toeing the red pile of the carpet

Doing hushed service

Each woman-of-the-people

Wearing a halo

A ludicrous little halo

Of which she is sublimely   unaware

I once heard in (Excerpt) a church

—Man and woman God made them—

                    Thank God.

The Black Maria: VIII (Excerpt)

Aracelis Girmay

The body, bearing something ordinary as light   Opens
as in a room somewhere the friend opens in poppy, in flame,
burns & bears the child — out.

When I did it was the hours & hours of breaking. The bucking
of it all, the push & head

not moving, not an inch until,
when he flew from me, it was the night who came

flying through me with all its hair,
the immense terror of his face & noise.

I heard the stranger & my brain, without looking, vowed
a love-him vow. His struggling, merely, to be

split me down, with the axe, to two. How true,
the thinness of our hovering between the realms of Here, Not
Here.

The fight, first, to open, then to breathe,
& then to close. Each of us entering the world

& entering the world like this.
Soft. Unlikely.   Then —

the idiosyncratic minds & verbs.
        Beloveds, making your ways

to & away from us, always, across the centuries,
inside the vastness of the galaxy, how improbable it is that this
iteration

of you or you or me might come to be at all — Body of fear,
Body of laughing — & even last a second. This fact should make
us fall all

to our knees with awe,
the beauty of it against these odds,

the stacks & stacks of near misses
& slimmest chances that birthed one ancestor into the next &
next.

Profound, unspeakable cruelty who counters this, who does not
see.

& so to tenderness I add my action.

We Cannot Sleep Alone

Emily Pérez

Between three and four we're lovers, four to five warriors, you

feast and linger at my breast, then reject me bodily. This latching

on then pulling back, gums clenched to nipple taffy. My body

made to feed and yours consume and gnash, dispense with me.

My son, my love, my tiny enemy.

Outside the New Body

Keetje Kuipers

One day I woke up in a new body

one that contained another and it made

      me dizzy Now you pull your hand from your

mouth as if to show me something   I've known

never

      Like those birds carrying mouthfuls

of steam all the stark winter months I held

you in my body   long as I could   Weighted

then with sadness too my fear

      you

might dissipate a fever brief and

      untethered as the man I saw dancing

wrapped in a bearskin rug head passing through

its teeth, its tender jaws I had never held

anyone so close

your eyes inside my

eyes tongue inside my tongue Now when I cup

your sleeping face against the bow of my

shoulder arrow notched I am just waiting

one more moment

before I let you go

I know the quiver of your heart is out-

side the inside of me What to do with

this new body you left behind the light

that streams through its too-thin walls of fraying silk?

The Poet Contemplates
the Nature of Motherhood

Jill Bialosky

He wants to know his history. It's not enough

to say *I am your mother. Your father is reading*

in the bedroom. He wants to know why

his eyes are blue-gray or sometimes green—

why her eyes are brown. He wants to understand

the lightness of his hair, the sensitivity of his skin,

why music is his language, not theirs.

This is your story, the poet says. *You were born a long time ago.*

You were a boy floating in a basket

on the Nile and I was a queen longing for a son

and your father was a king come to claim you

from the water. No, he says. You're lying. Why are the leaves

falling? When will it snow? Do you think the boy will find

her again, the woman who cast him out alone?

How did she know he wouldn't drown?

But he's not alone, she says.

Self Portrait in the Backyard as Mother

Nicole Cooley

Tulip-bellied, fists full of weeds, the baby shuffles over the wet grass,

the baby stumbles like a drunk

toward me, the baby wants to roll on top of me,

climb back inside my body but what about

the times I want her gone, want my body to myself,

want only to believe in my own useless wanting?

[Sleep, darling]

Sappho, translated by Mary Barnard

Sleep, darling

I have a small

daughter called

Cleis, who is

like a golden

flower

        I wouldn't

take all Croesus'

kingdom with love

thrown in, for her

Motherload

Kate Baer

She keeps an office in her sternum, the flat

bone in the center of her chest with all its

urgent papers, vast appointments, lists of

minor things. In her vertebra she holds more

carnal tasks; milk jugs, rotten plants, heavy-

bottomed toddlers in all their mortal rage.

She keeps frustration in her hallux: senseless

chatter, jealous fangs, the spikes of a dinosaur's

tail. The belly is more complicated—all heartache

and ambition. Fires and tidal waves.

In her pelvis she holds her labors, long and slippery. In her clavicle, silent things. (Money and power. Safety and choice. Tiny banquets of shame.)

In her hands she carries their egos, small and flimsy. In her mouth she holds her laughter, gentle currents, a cosmos of everything.

In the Horniman Museum

Clare Pollard

In South London, on a Sunday,

we have seen the scratching chickens

and alpacas being spitty

when the rain drives us indoors

where the taxidermy's waiting

and you race around glass coffins,

the hummingbirds in friezes,

Vulpes vulpes and the *Cervus*

posed as if in toyshop windows

and the walrus like a punchline.

Relation of *Pan troglodytes*,

you're animal, as they are,

each captured by a caption

in a tea trader's collection.

He paid to have the world paused:

all those thousand conscious seeings

for one vision! All that *I am*

turned to glaze for one man's gaze.

I've not told you about death yet.

Can you tell these birds are different?

Do you think this heron cruel,

that he doesn't care about you?

It's true. The heron doesn't.

Caring's something rare and fleeting

(if the dead see anything

then it's as hard and black as glass.)

But your eyes are getting rounder,

pointing 'dere!' at crocs and gibbons

and the peacock's staring blueness,

and we're falling through our days

in this pissing useless ark

while the clouds gather like stuffing,

while the floodwater ticks upwards.

My child, you are an *I* —

through your two eyes, not yet dark,

can you see your we-cheeked mother

and the whole creaturely Kingdom

that is stood today before you

in its opulence and armour,

that has held its breath this moment

and is waiting for your judgement?

Prayer

Jennifer Givhan

When I lost you at the market, I cleared

each shelf for your folded little boy body

(what was it you loved in hide and seek?

the brief escape, the minutes you didn't belong

to me, when no one could find you until)

I found you with a muumuu'd woman

hunkered between shopping carts. You'd gifted

her your animal crackers for offering you

a prayer. My son, performing miracles

every time you wash your feet or clean your

plate of fish sticks, my heart cliff-dives

when I find you weeping for a classmate

or alone in the yard watching a cloud

rising from the river, so when I grabbed your

little body, hugged you, took in your scent

of sweat and cookies and dirt, I swore I'd

never lose you again. My cheeks hot

against yours, I wondered if you knew my

only prayer, whispered nightly: *God, if you*

ask me to let him go, I'll say fuck no.

A Fable

Louise Glück

Two women with

the same claim

came to the feet of

the wise king. Two women,

but only one baby.

The king knew

someone was lying.

What he said was

Let the child be

cut in half; that way

no one will go

empty-handed. He

drew his sword.

Then, of the two

women, one

renounced her share:

this was

the sign, the lesson.

Suppose

you saw your mother

torn between two daughters:

what could you do

to save her but be

willing to destroy

yourself—she would know

who was the rightful child,

the one who couldn't bear

to divide the mother.

Waterwings

Cathy Song

The mornings are his,

blue and white

like the tablecloth at breakfast.

He's happy in the house,

a sweep of the spoon

brings the birds under his chair.

He sings and the dishes disappear.

Or holding a crayon like a candle,

he draws a circle.

It is his hundredth dragonfly.

Calling for more paper,

this one is red-winged

and like the others,

he wills it to fly, simply

by the unformed curve of his signature.

Waterwings he calls them,

the floats I strap to his arms.

I wear an apron of concern,

sweep the morning of birds.

To the water he returns,

plunging where it's cold,

moving and squealing into sunlight.

The water from here seems flecked with gold.

I watch the circles

his small body makes

fan and ripple,

disperse like an echo

into the sum of water, light and air.

His imprint on the water

has but a brief lifespan,

the flicker of a dragonfly's delicate wing.

This is sadness, I tell myself,

the morning he chooses to leave his wings behind,

because he will not remember

that he and beauty were aligned,

skimming across the water, nearly airborne,

on his first solo flight.

I'll write "how he could not

contain his delight."

At the other end,

in another time frame,

he waits for me—

having already outdistanced this body,

the one that slipped from me like a fish,

floating, free of itself.

I Want the World

Brenda Shaughnessy

You never know, when you say goodbye, if it's the last time.
Last time for who? For what?

Every time is the last—for that particular goodbye, wearing
those clothes, at that airport. Me in my black dress-nightgown,
fifties housecoat, funeral uniform. It passes for anything.

My daughter in her fuchsia track shorts and faded green t-shirt
almost as soft as her luscious little arms. She was complaining,
as usual. She was hungry. She was tired of traveling.

Her complaints were especially unpleasant since they only
pointed up how innocent she was of how bad everything could
get. The Legos are boring? Imagine no toys of any kind.

The chicken nuggets are too hot? Just wait. They'll cool and
by then, I hope she can learn to like lizard blood and shoelace
chewing gum, because that's what's coming.

A fierce zip of pride bites my heart. She demands more because she knows there's more in the world and she believes she should have it all. She knows what she wants: what she wants.

She believes the world is coming to her, not veering definitively away. She still thinks we can choose between ice cream flavors, bless her that she has so many possible flavors in mind.

Between stuffed animals and dolls. Which color lunch box you want for the whole school year. What school year? I think. Will first grade exist this coming fall?

She still thinks that what she thinks will affect what she gets. She still believes tantrums might get her her way. She doesn't know yet that nobody gets her way.

We're all lucky if we get anything at all, come dinnertime, come night, the next morning and the next hot morning, the next endangered livingspace if we get to stay there. We can't carry all that stuff. But she doesn't think of it as stuff.

She thinks of it as what she wants. Life's been consistent—me resisting her demands, me in my black dress, cutting my hair to make her paintbrushes. If something happens to me, who will help her believe her beliefs?

She believes her desires—as erratic and irrational as a six-year-old's desires can be—nevertheless have intrinsic value. A thread of hope wound, inextricable, all around and through her very person. I believe that, too.

One of these mornings I'll say goodbye, a routine goodbye when I go to the FedPlex warehouse to work or pick my rations, and in my absence she will lose that thread, come to fully understand what she wants is impossible in our world.

All of it, any of it, the tiniest thing, impossible.

I won't have known but I'll be walking away from my daughter for the last time, coming home (wherever home is) to someone new, someone broken off from my old girl, six years old.

Here, I tell her, providing a pencil with a pristine, unsharpened end, chew on this. Nobody's touched it yet. It's all yours, darling.

Somewhere I'll find a blade to sharpen it, and we'll find a scrap for drawing, a bit of napkin or a smooth, light stone. For now, you can chew on it. Soon you'll be able to draw whatever you want.

She, As Painter

Tina Chang

I sing a song to my children.

If I sing it just right, it is greater

than a psalm. It is a hilltop.

It is thunder. My daughter finds me

in the bed sleeping, she places

her head to my chest.

One beat. A leap. Slow listening.

When my stepfather was alive

judgment was beast inside his mouth.

When he died, I was relieved.

No more of his laughter beside me

at the childhood table. No more slaughter.

My daughter worries and shakes me awake.

Until I reassure her my living

is living inside her too.

I place her in the bed with me

where she sinks into the mattress.

I dream her fear and dream her safety

simultaneously slithering down

a tree. I smooth down the curls

of her hair, the waves of which

are now holding up a boat.

We sit together bobbing.

She feels she has painted

the sky's complication.

We are changed by their hue,

and their shifting lumen. I can't take

this love I feel. The waters rise up

and I assure her the water will not spill

into the boat. Water teeters at the edge.

The Daughter

Carmen Giménez Smith

We said she was a negative image of me because of her lightness.

She's light and also passage, the glory in my cortex.

Daughter, where did you get all that goddess?

Her eyes are Neruda's two dark pools at twilight.

Sometimes she's a stranger in my home because I hadn't imagined her.

Who will her daughter be?

She and I are the gradual ebb of my mother's darkness.

I unfurl the ribbon of her life, and it's a smooth long hallway, doors flung open.

Her surface is a deflection is why.

Harm on her, harm on us all.

Inside her, my grit and timbre, my reckless.

Hours Days Years Unmoor Their Orbits

Rachel Zucker

tonight I'm cleaning baby portobellos

for you, my young activist

wiping the dirty tops with a damp cloth

as carefully as I used to rinse raspberries

for you to adorn your fingertips

before eating each blood-red prize

these days you rarely look me in the eye

& your long shagged hair hides your smile

I don't expect you to remember or

understand the many ways I've kept you

alive or the life my love for you

has made me live

Mother's Day

David Young

—for my children

I see her doing something simple, paying bills,

or leafing through a magazine or book,

and wish that I could say, and she could hear,

that now I start to understand her love

for all of us, the fullness of it.

It burns there in the past, beyond my reach,

a modest lamp.

The Real Reason

Ada Limón

I don't have any tattoos is not my story to tell. It's my

mother's. Once, walking down Bedford Avenue in my twenties,

I called her as I did, as I do. I told her how I wanted a tattoo

on the back of my neck. Something minor, but permanent,

and she is an artist, I wanted her to create the design, a symbol,

a fish I dream of every night. An underwater talisman,
a mother's

gift on my body. To be clear, I thought she'd be honored.
But do we

ever really know each other fully? A silence like a hospital
room; she

was in tears. I swore then that I wouldn't get one. Wouldn't let a needle

touch my neck, my arm, my torso. I'd stay me, my skin the skin

she welcomed me into the world with. It wasn't until later that

I knew it wasn't so much the tattoo, but the marking, the idea

of scars. What you don't know (and this is why this is not my story)

is that my mother is scarred from burns over a great deal of her body.

Most from an explosion that took her first child she was carrying

in her belly, others from the skin grafts where they took skin to cover what needed it. She was in her late twenties when that happened.

Outside her studio in the center of town. You have to understand,

my mother is beautiful. Tall and elegant, thin and strong. I have not

known her any other way, her skin that I mapped with my young

fingers, its strange hardness in places, its patterns like quilts here,

riverbeds there. She's wondrous, preternatural, survived fire, the ending of an unborn child. Heat and flame and death, all made

her into something seemingly magical, a phoenixess. What I know

now is she wanted something else for me. For me to wake each

morning and recognize my own flesh, for this one thing she made—

me—to remain how she intended, for one of us

to make it out unscathed.

The courage that my mother had

Edna St. Vincent Millay

The courage that my mother had

Went with her, and is with her still:

Rock from New England quarried;

Now granite in a granite hill.

The golden brooch my mother wore

She left behind for me to wear;

I have no thing I treasure more:

Yet, it is something I could spare.

Oh, if instead she'd left to me

The thing she took into the grave!—

That courage like a rock, which she

Has no more need of, and I have.

my mama moved among the days

Lucille Clifton

my mama moved among the days

like a dreamwalker in a field;

seemed like what she touched was hers

seemed like what touched her couldn't hold,

she got us almost through the high grass

then seemed like she turned around and ran

right back in

right back on in

Foreign Body

Kimiko Hahn

This is a poem on my other's body,

I mean, my mother's body, I mean the one

who saved her braid of blue-black hair

in a drawer when I was little.

Meaning one I could lean against —

against not in resistance. Fuzzy dress

of wuzzy one. Red lipstick one.

Kitchen one. Her one to me,

bad-ger bad-ger —

or so I heard. The one body I write on

like Daddy's blank studio wall

with my colored pencils.

About seeing her skin

as she bathed in the afternoon —

was I five? It was summer.

Then today's winter where again

I call that bath to mind.

I cannot leave her body alone.

Which is how I found Mother in the bath

escaping the heat of a 1950s house,

Father on a ladder with blowtorch

to scrape the paint off the outside.

•

badger badger

•

The sun in the suburbs

simmered the tar roof over our rooms

in the, town where only wasps lived

inside paper cells beneath eaves and roots.

And they hurt very much, the wasps.

•

Now I am sixty. Sweet as dried papaya.

My hair, a bit tarnished,

my inmost, null.

Memory is failing away

as if an image shattered to shards then

recollected for a kaleidoscope:

I click the pieces into sharp arrangements —

grouse, crow, craven

— no, now, my own daughter turns sovereign

Legacies

Nikki Giovanni

her grandmother called her from the playground

    "yes, ma'am"

    "i want chu to learn how to make rolls" said the old

woman proudly

but the little girl didn't want

to learn how because she knew

even if she couldn't say it that

that would mean when the old one died she would be less

dependent on her spirit so

she said

"i don't want to know how to make no rolls"

with her lips poked out

and the old woman wiped her hands on

her apron saying "lord

these children"

and neither of them ever

said what they meant

and i guess nobody ever does

Nature, the gentlest mother

Emily Dickinson

Nature, the gentlest mother

Impatient of no child,

The feeblest or the waywardest,—

Her admonition mild

In forest and the hill

By traveller is heard,

Restraining rampant squirrel

Or too impetuous bird.

How fair her conversation,

A summer afternoon,—

Her household, her assembly;

And when the sun goes down

Her voice among the aisles

Incites the timid prayer

Of the minutest cricket,

The most unworthy flower.

When all the children sleep

She turns as long away

As will suffice to light her lamps;

Then, bending from the sky,

With infinite affection

And infiniter care,

Her golden finger on her lip,

Wills silence everywhere.

Credits